KENYA

Ali Brownlie

Photographs by Chris Fairclough

CHERRYTREE BOOKS

LETTERS FROM AROUND THE WORLD

Titles in this series

BANGLADESH · BRAZIL · CHINA · FRANCE · INDIA · ITALY · JAMAICA · JAPAN · KENYA · SPAIN

A Cherrytree Book

Conceived and produced by

Nutshell MEDIA

Intergen House
65-67 Western Road
Hove BN3 2JQ, UK
www.nutshellmedialtd.co.uk

First published by
Evans Brothers Ltd
2A Portman Mansions
Chiltern Street
London W1U 6NR

VISIT OUR WEBSITE
www.evansbooks.co.uk

Reprinted 2006
Editor: Katie Orchard
Designer: Tim Mayer
Map artwork: Encompass Graphics Ltd
All other artwork: Tim Mayer
Geography consultant: Jeff Stanfield, County Inspector
    for Geography, Hampshire LEA
Literacy consultant: Anne Spiring

All photographs were taken by Chris Fairclough.

Printed in China

Acknowledgements
The photographer would like to thank the following for
their help with this book: The Ngatia family and the staff and
pupils of the Milimani Primary School, near Naivasha.

British Library Cataloguing in Publication Data
Brownlie, Alison, 1949-
    Kenya. – (Letters from around the world)
    1. Kenya - Social conditions - 1963 - Juvenile literature
    2. Kenya - Social life and customs - 20th century -
    Juvenile literature
    I. Title
    967.6'2'042

ISBN 1842341448
13-digit ISBN (from 1 Jan 2007) 978 1 84234 144 5

Cover: Fred and some of his footballing friends.
Title page: Sugar-cane is a tasty treat.
This page: Boys having fun in Lake Naivasha.
Contents page: Fred rides his dad's tractor.
Glossary page: Fred catches the *matatu* to school.
Further information page: Washing clothes in Lake Naivasha.
Index: Zebras dry off after a downpour.

Contents

My Country

Tuesday, 8 January

PO Box 345
Naivasha
Kenya

Dear Alex,

Jambo! (This means 'hi' in Swahili.)

My name's Fred Ngatia and I'm 9 years old. I live in a village called Karagita, near Naivasha, in Kenya. (You can see Karagita and Naivasha on the map opposite.) I have three brothers, Patrick, Peter and Gabriel, and one sister, Selma. I hope I can help you with your class projects on Kenya.

Write back soon!

From

Fred

This is me on my bike. Mum is wearing green. Dad is next to her. The others are my brothers, sister and cousins.

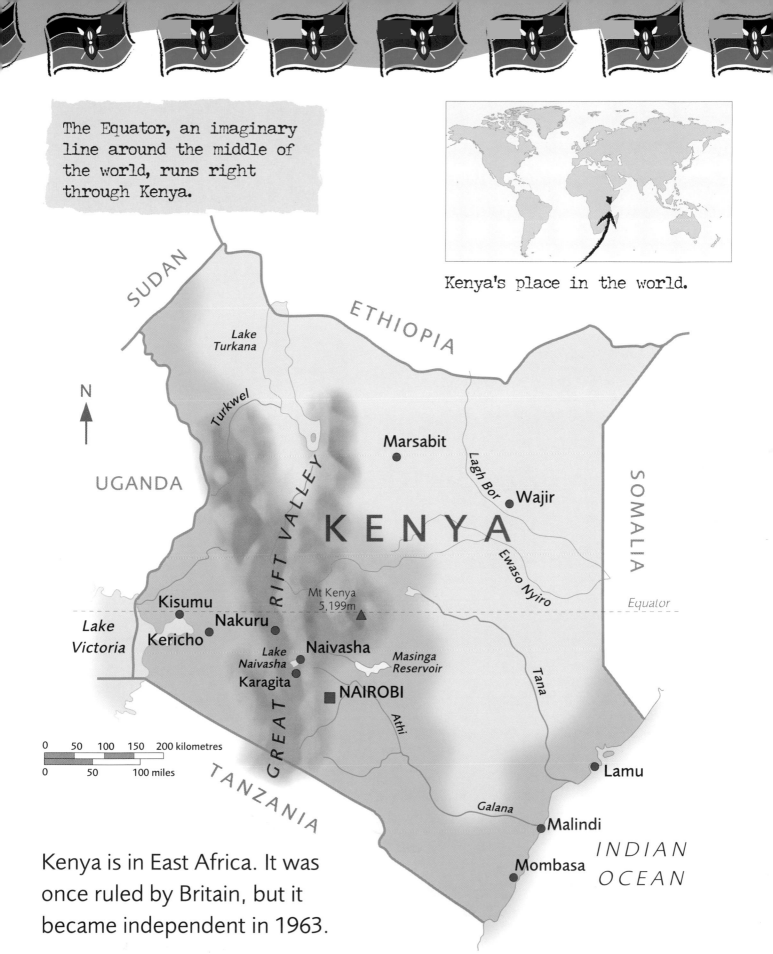

The Equator, an imaginary line around the middle of the world, runs right through Kenya.

Kenya's place in the world.

Kenya is in East Africa. It was once ruled by Britain, but it became independent in 1963.

Karagita is a small village about 6 kilometres from Naivasha. Naivasha is a popular holiday town with several hotels. It takes about 2 hours to drive to Naivasha from Kenya's capital city, Nairobi.

There are many small farms and villages in the hilly countryside around Naivasha.

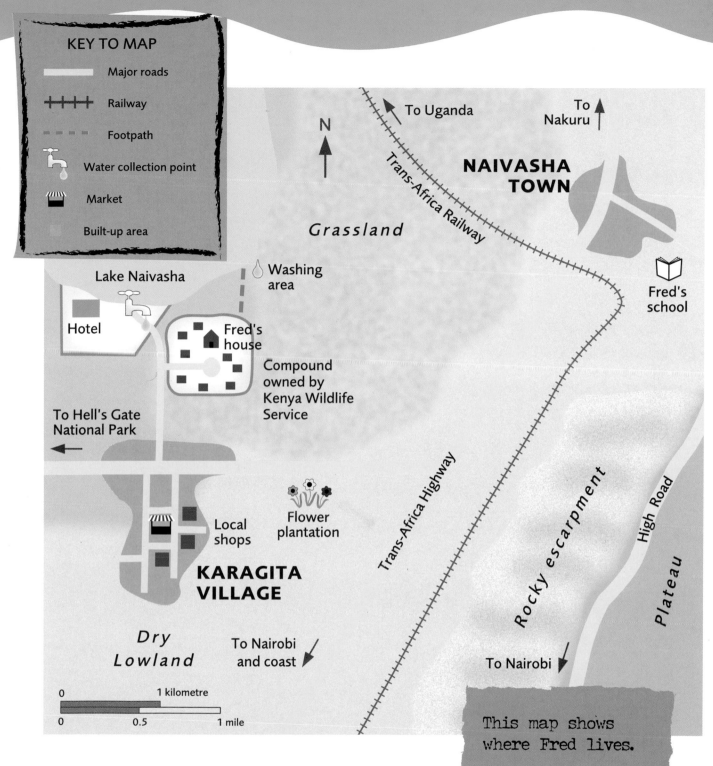

KEY TO MAP

——	Major roads
+-+-+-+	Railway
- - - -	Footpath
🚰	Water collection point
🏪	Market
▨	Built-up area

To Uganda

To Nakuru

NAIVASHA TOWN

Trans-Africa Railway

Grassland

N

Lake Naivasha

Washing area

Hotel

Fred's house

Compound owned by Kenya Wildlife Service

Fred's school

To Hell's Gate National Park

Flower plantation

Local shops

Trans-Africa Highway

Rocky escarpment

High Road

KARAGITA VILLAGE

Plateau

Dry Lowland

To Nairobi and coast

To Nairobi

0	1 kilometre
0	0.5	1 mile

This map shows where Fred lives.

Karagita is on the shore of Lake Naivasha.
Many beautiful birds, such as pelicans and
flamingos, live on the lake. Tourists from all over
the world come to Lake Naivasha to see the birds
in their natural habitat.

Landscape and Weather

Naivasha is in the Great Rift Valley, a valley that stretches for over 6,500 kilometres through East Africa. The area around Lake Naivasha is a national park. There are wild buffalo, zebras, giraffes, lions and leopards.

These zebras are drying off after some heavy rain.

On hot days, a swim in the lake is cool and refreshing.

Naivasha's Climate

January	July
Temperature	Temperature
18°C	17°C
38mm	43mm
Rainfall	Rainfall

Some parts of Kenya can be very hot, but Naivasha has a temperate climate. This means that it is neither very hot nor very cold. The temperature does not change much from summer to winter. It rains most heavily in April and May.

At Home

Fred's house is part of a small group of houses, called a compound. His aunts and uncles live in the other houses. The compound is like a small village. Everybody helps each other.

Fred and Peter do their homework in their bedroom.

Fred's house has four bedrooms, a kitchen and a living room. Fred shares a bedroom with his older brother, Peter, who is 10.

The house is made from concrete blocks. It has a corrugated-iron roof, which is noisy when it rains. There is no running water or electricity.

Fred's family relaxes together in the living room.

All the families in the compound wash their clothes beside the lake.

Every day Fred's mum chops wood to use on the fire for cooking.

Most families in the compound own a small plot of land, called a *shamba*. Here they grow maize and sweet potatoes. They grow just enough to feed the family. Fred's family's *shamba* is about 6 kilometres away from their house.

Water has to be carried from the nearest tap, which is about 500 metres away.

Wednesday, 13 March

PO Box 345
Naivasha
Kenya

Dear Alex,

Do you grow any food at home? We do. Every weekend someone in my family, usually my mother, goes to our *shamba*. Mum looks after the crops and does the weeding with a hoe. When it's time to harvest the vegetables, we all go to help.

My dad has a tractor. I'm allowed to drive it sometimes. I could teach you to drive it if you ever came to Kenya!

From

Fred

This is me on our tractor. I want to be a truck driver when I'm older.

Food and Mealtimes

Fred and his sister
Selma help their mum
buy fresh vegetables
at the market.

Fred's family cannot grow everything they need to eat
on the *shamba*. Some fruit and vegetables come from
the market in Karagita.

Fred wakes up at 5 a.m. For breakfast he has a *chapatti*, a type of bread, and some sweet tea. Sometimes he has an egg.

Kenyan food includes dishes from other countries. *Samosas*, small spicy pasties that came from India, are sold at roadside stalls.

Sugar-cane is a popular, tasty snack.

Fred's family has a few chickens. His brother Patrick feeds them and collects their eggs.

The family eats a meal of *sukuma wiki* and *ugali*.

When Fred comes home from school, the whole family sits down together to eat the main meal of the day. Often this is *sukuma wiki*, a cabbage stew that is cheap to cook and very healthy. It is usually eaten with *ugali*. This is like mashed potato, made from maize meal.

Beef stew, known as *nyama choma*, is a popular dish found all over Kenya.

Saturday, 3 May

PO Box 345
Naivasha
Kenya

Jambo Alex!

Thanks for your letter. You wanted to know what my favourite food is – it's *sukuma wiki*. Here's how to make it:

You will need: 2 tablespoons of oil, 1 chopped onion, 2 chopped tomatoes, 500g chopped cabbage, pinch of salt, $\frac{1}{2}$ teaspoon of chilli powder, 6 tablespoons of water, 3 tablespoons of lemon juice.

1. Fry the onions in the oil for about 5 minutes, until they are soft.
2. Add the tomatoes and the cabbage.
3. Add the water, the salt and the chilli powder.
4. Simmer for 10 minutes until the cabbage is cooked through.
5. Add some lemon juice to taste, then serve. (We eat it with *ugali*, but you could try it with mashed potato.)

Let me know what you think of it.

From

Fred

Mum puts some chopped cabbage in the pan.

School Day

Every school day, Fred puts on his school uniform and sets off for Milimani Primary School, 6 kilometres away. Fred, his brothers and his sister walk to the bus stop. Then they catch the *matatu*, which is a public mini-bus.

Matatus are a cheap and quick way of getting around in Kenya.

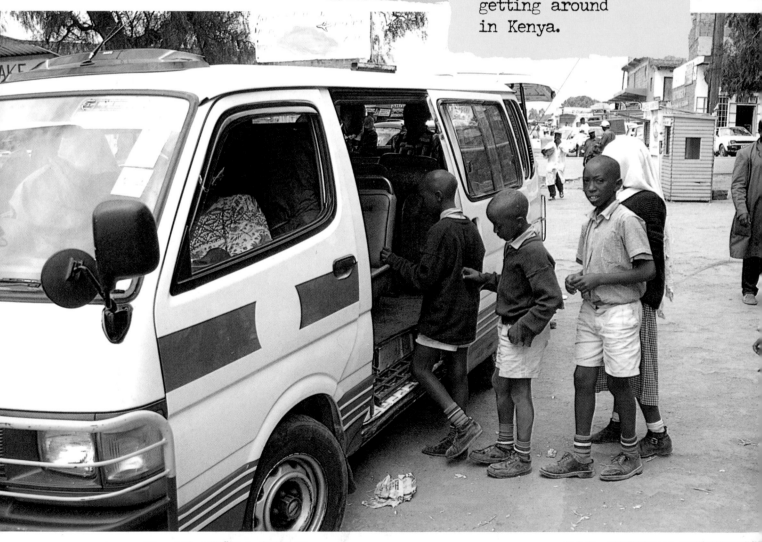

In Kenya, all parents have to pay for their children's education. Some children have to stay at home because their parents cannot afford to send them to school.

Fred is lucky. He enjoys school and thinks it is very important to learn.

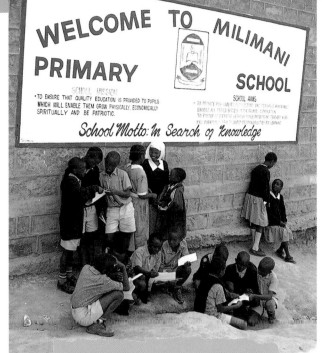

Children catch up with their friends before school begins, at 8.45 a.m.

Often the weather is warm enough to have lessons outside.

19

Fred and his classmates are hard at work in an English lesson.

The school day finishes at 4 p.m. Younger children sometimes finish earlier than this. Fred has been going to school since he was 5 years old. When he is 12, he will go to the secondary school in Naivasha.

At the prize-giving ceremony, the head teacher proudly carries the top student in front of the whole school.

Friday, 19 July

PO Box 345
Naivasha
Kenya

Dear Alex,

Thanks for your letter. I'm glad you tried my recipe!
Today was the last day of term. Mum and Dad seemed
quite pleased with my school report. I did well in English,
which is my favourite subject. I also study geography,
history, arts and crafts, maths, science, religious studies
and Swahili.

We speak Swahili
at home but at
school we're supposed
to speak in English.
Can you speak any
other languages?

From

Fred

↗

Here I am showing
Mum and Dad my
report. I was very
nervous!

Off to Work

Fred's dad is a park ranger. One of his jobs is to check the water levels in Lake Naivasha. People are using too much water from the lake and it is getting smaller.

Fred's dad works for the Kenya Wildlife Service. Here he is at his office.

Some Kenyan people work in the tourist industry as tour guides or in the hotels. Others work on plantations growing crops for export, such as tea, coffee or flowers.

Freshly picked tea
is weighed at a
plantation in Kericho.

The land around
Naivasha is very fertile.
Farmers use water from
the lake to help their
crops grow. Many flowers
are grown in the area and
exported to Europe.

A woman picks flowers for
export. They are picked
before they have opened
so that they last longer.

Free Time

Fred catches a ride on the back of his brother's bike.

There is always something to be done at home or on the *shamba*. When Fred is not helping with the chores, he enjoys swimming in the lake or playing football with his friends.

Football is Fred's favourite sport.

Saturday, 7 September

PO Box 345
Naivasha
Kenya

Jambo Alex!

It's the weekend here and I'm going out to play with my friends. What do you do in your spare time? I love to play football with the other kids in the compound.

Toys and games are expensive. We make our own from things we find lying around. Our home-made toys don't always last very long, but it's easy to make some more.

Do you ever make your own games?

From

Fred

We've made a football from some old bags tied round with string.

Religion and Special Days

Children at Fred's school say prayers each morning.

Most people in Kenya are Christians. Fred and his family go to church every Sunday.

There are also Muslims and Hindus. Most of the people who live on the coast are Muslims.

On her wedding day, a Kenyan bride is carried out of the house by the women in her family.

One important celebration for people of all religions is Kenyatta Day on 20 October. Jomo Kenyatta was Kenya's first president. Kenyatta Day is a national holiday and no one goes to work or school.

A Christian wedding. It is traditional for the bride to wear a white dress.

Fact File

Population: 30.3 million.

Flag: Kenya became independent on 12 December 1963. The colours of Kenya's flag have special meanings: black for the people, green for the land, red for the price of freedom and white for peace. The shield is for protection.

Capital city: The capital of Kenya is Nairobi. It has a population of 2.1 million. Nairobi has modern skyscrapers as well as much older buildings with walls made from mud. It is 1,800m above sea-level.

Other major cities: Nakuru, Mombasa (a major port on the Indian Ocean and an important tourist destination), Kisumu (a port on Lake Victoria).

Neighbouring countries: Ethiopia, Somalia, Tanzania, Uganda and Sudan.

Size: 582,650km².

Motto: Kenya's motto is *Harambee*, which means 'Pull together'.

Kenyan stamps: Kenyan stamps often show wildlife or details of Kenyan life such as tourism and culture. These stamps show important crops grown in Kenya.

Languages: English and Swahili are the official languages. There are more than 40 local ethnic languages.

Currency: The currency is the Kenyan shilling. There are 100 cents in a shilling. There is often a picture of the Kenyan president on the bank notes.

Highest mountain: The highest point is Mount Kenya at 5,199m. It is the second-highest mountain in Africa and lies on the Equator.

Main industries: Tea, coffee and sugar production and tourism are all important industries in Kenya.

Wildlife: Kenya's wildlife is world famous. Tourists go on safari to see animals such as lions, leopards, rhinos, elephants and giraffes.

Main religions: In Kenya 38 per cent of the population are Protestant, 28 per cent are Roman Catholic, 26 per cent follow local beliefs, and 8 per cent follow Islam, Hinduism or other religions.

Longest river: The Tana River is 1,014km long.

Glossary

compound A small group of houses sharing facilities such as water.

corrugated iron Sheets of wavy iron often used for roofing.

Equator An imaginary line that goes around the middle of the Earth.

exports Goods that are sold to another country.

fertile Soil that is good for growing plants.

habitat The place where plants and animals live.

maize A tall cereal crop with yellow kernels. In Britain it is called corn.

national park An area of land where wildlife is protected.

plantation A large farm where just one crop is grown for export.

running water Water that is supplied through pipes and taps.

shamba The Swahili word for a small plot of land, where a family grows enough food for themselves.

sukuma wiki A type of cabbage stew.

Swahili Along with English, this is the official language in Kenya.

temperate climate A weather system that is neither very hot, nor very cold.

ugali A side-dish, like mashed potato. It is made from maize and is eaten with most meals.

Further Information

Information books:

A Flavour of Kenya by Wambui Kairi (Hodder Wayland, 1999)

We Come from Kenya by Wambui Kairi (Hodder Wayland, 1999)

Worldfocus: Kenya by David Marshall and Geoff Sayer (Heinemann/Oxfam, 1996)

Fiction:

Bringing the Rains to Kapiti Plain by Verna Aardema, illustrated by Beatriz Vidal (Macmillan Children's Books, 1986). A nursery rhyme telling the story of how a young herd boy ended a dreadful drought.

Mcheshi Goes on a Journey, *Mcheshi Goes to the Game Park* and *Mcheshi Goes to the Market* illustrated by Judy Wanjiku Mathenge and Robin Miranda (Jacaranda Designs Ltd, 1993). Dual-language books available worldwide.

Resource packs:

Feeling Good About Faraway Friends: Daily Life of a Maasai Family in Kenya (Leeds DEC, 1996)

Websites:

CIA World Factbook
www.cia.gov/cia/publications/factbook/
Basic facts and figures about Kenya and other countries.

Kenya Wildlife Service
www.kenya-wildlife-service.org
Information about Kenya's wildlife.

Bwana Zulia's Kenya Travel Guide
www.bwanazulia.com/swahili.html
An introduction to Swahili, including words for food and drink.

Joe the Dragon's Kenya Page
www.joethedragon.co.uk/kenya.html
Fun website with games and photos.

Index